CONTENTS

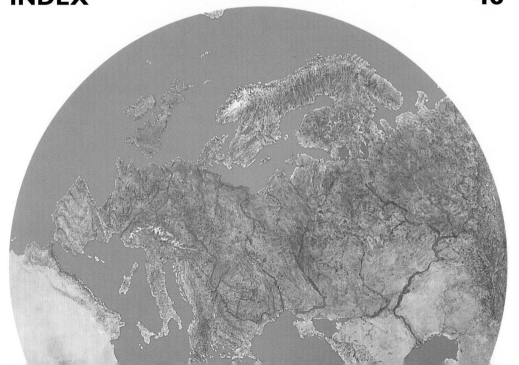

EUROPE BY COUNTRY

NORTH-WEST EUROPE

The countries of north-west Europe are linked closely together economically, and co-operate in other ways; they are generally wealthy countries, enjoying a high standard of living. The most northerly countries straddle the Arctic Circle, but those further south have moderate climates with cold winters and warm summers.

FINLAND
Capital: Helsinki
Area: 338,145 km²
Population: 5,154,400
Currency: Markka
GNP per person (US$): 24,790
Principal languages: Finnish, Swedish

ICELAND
Capital: Reykjavik
Area: 103,000 km²
Population: 276,000
Currency: Krona
GNP per person (US$): 26,470
Principal languages: Icelandic

NORWAY
Capital: Oslo
Area: 323,378 km²
Population: 4,419,000
Currency: Krone
GNP per person (US$): 36,100
Principal languages: Norwegian

SWEDEN
Capital: Stockholm
Area: 444,964 km²
Population: 8,875,000
Currency: Swedish Krona
GNP per person (US$): 26,210
Principal languages: Swedish

UNITED KINGDOM
Capital: London
Area: 244,100 km²
Population: 58,649,000
Currency: Pound
GNP per person (US$): 20,870
Principal languages: English, Welsh, Gaelic

DENMARK
Capital: Copenhagen
Area: 43,092 km²
Population: 5,270,000
Currency: Danish Krone
GNP per person (US$): 34,890
Principal languages: Danish, Faerose

EIRE
Capital: Dublin
Area: 70,283 km²
Population: 3,681,000
Currency: Irish Punt
GNP per person (US$): 17,790
Principal languages: Irish, English

BELGIUM
Capital: Brussels
Area: 30,519 km²
Population: 10,141,000
Currency: Belgian Franc
GNP per person (US$): 26,730
Principal languages: Flemish, French

FRANCE
Capital: Paris
Area: 543,965 km²
Population: 58,683,000
Currency: French Franc
GNP per person (US$): 26,300
Principal languages: French (Breton and Basque minorities)

LUXEMBOURG
Capital: Luxembourg
Area: 2,586 km²
Population: 422,000
Currency: Luxembourg Franc
GNP per person (US$): 44,690
Principal languages: Letzeburgish, French

GERMANY
Capital: Berlin
Area: 356,945 km²
Population: 82,133,000
Currency: Deutschmark
GNP per person (US$): 28,280
Principal languages: German

AUSTRIA
Capital: Vienna
Area: 83,853 km²
Population: 8,140,000
Currency: Schilling
GNP per person (US$): 27,920
Principal languages: German

NETHERLANDS
Capital: Amsterdam
Area: 41,863 km²
Population: 15,678,000
Currency: Guilder or Florin
GNP per person (US$): 25,830
Principal languages: Dutch

MONACO
Capital: Monaco
Area: 1.8 km²
Population: 33,000
Currency: French Franc
GNP per person (US$): 11,000
Principal languages: French, Monegasque

SWITZERLAND
Capital: Bern
Area: 41,288 km²
Population: 7,299,000
Currency: Swiss Franc
GNP per person (US$): 43,060
Principal languages: German, French, Italian, Romansch

LIECHTENSTEIN
Capital: Vaduz
Area: 160 km²
Population: 32,000
Currency: Swiss Franc
GNP per person (US$): 33,510
Principal languages: German

0   200   400   600   800 km
0 100 200 300 400 500 miles

Map labels:
Reykjavik, ICELAND, SWEDEN, FINLAND, Helsinki, NORWAY, Oslo, Stockholm, DENMARK, Copenhagen, NORTHERN IRELAND, Dublin, UNITED KINGDOM, EIRE, NETHERLANDS, Amsterdam, Berlin, London, Brussels, BELGIUM, GERMANY, Paris, LUXEMBOURG, Vienna, AUSTRIA, FRANCE, Bern, SWITZERLAND, LIECHTENSTEIN, MONACO

CONTINENTS

EUROPE

Ewan McLeish

HODDER
Wayland

an imprint of Hodder Children's Books

CONTINENTS series includes:

AFRICA
AUSTRALIA & OCEANIA

EUROPE
NORTH AMERICA

First published in Great Britain in 1996 by Wayland Publishers
Ltd. This updated paperback edition published in 2000 by
Hodder Wayland, an imprint of Hodder Children's Books.

A Catalogue record for this book is available from the
British Library.

ISBN 0 7502 2836 9

Printed and bound in Italy by G. Canale & C. S.p.A..

Hodder Children's Books
A division of Hodder Headline plc
338 Euston Road, London NW1 3BH

Statistics
Population figures in this book are for 1998.
GNP per capita are for 1997.

Sources
Eurostat, 1995
United Nations Development Programme
Unicef: *The State of the World's Children, 2000*

Picture Acknowledgements
Cover; All Sports 26; Britstock-IFA 14, 37; Camera Press 16, 35;
Format 22; Gamma 21, 34; Hulton Deutsch 18, 19; Hutchinson
20, 42; Impact 40; Image Bank 23, 27; Military Picture Library
43; Panos 40; Dr. J. Rowe 41; Science Photo Library 1, 3, 9, 12,
39; Trip 8, 10, 11, 13, 25, 29, 30, 31, 32, 33, 35, 36, 38; Zefa 26.

Maps by Peter Bull
Graph artwork by Mark Whitchurch
Printed and bound in Italy by G Canale

CENTRAL AND EASTERN EUROPE

The countries of central and eastern Europe were under communist control until 1989-1990. Their economies were mainly owned and controlled by the state. Following the collapse of communism, these countries moved rapidly towards a capitalist or free-market economy and democratic government. Most East Europeans still have a relatively low standard of living, but now enjoy freedoms of action and speech and other opportunities that were not possible under communism. However, they have also 'inherited' many of Western Europe's problems, including high unemployment, increasing social inequality and soaring crime rates.

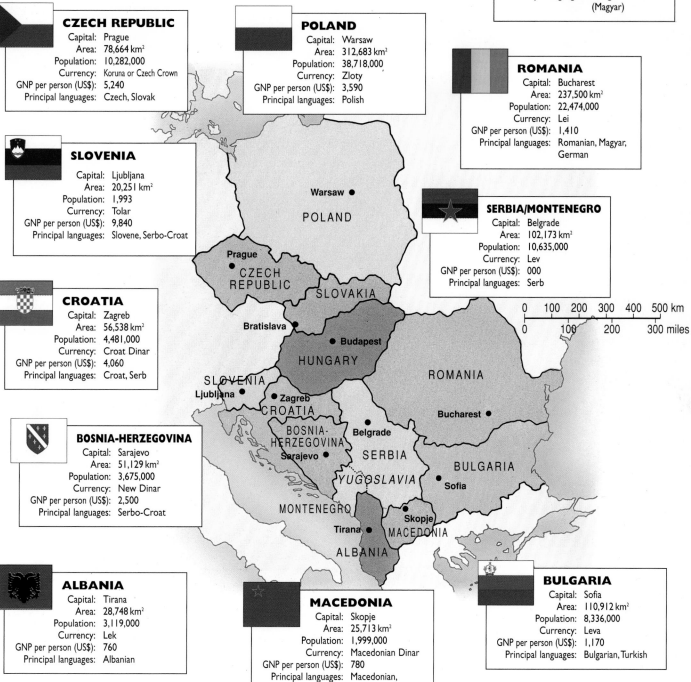

SLOVAKIA
Capital: Bratislava
Area: 49,035 km²
Population: 5,377,000
Currency: Slovak Koruna
GNP per person (US$): 3,680
Principal languages: Slovak, Magyar

HUNGARY
Capital: Budapest
Area: 93,030 km²
Population: 10,116,000
Currency: Forint
GNP per person (US$): 4,510
Principal languages: Hungarian (Magyar)

CZECH REPUBLIC
Capital: Prague
Area: 78,664 km²
Population: 10,282,000
Currency: Koruna or Czech Crown
GNP per person (US$): 5,240
Principal languages: Czech, Slovak

POLAND
Capital: Warsaw
Area: 312,683 km²
Population: 38,718,000
Currency: Zloty
GNP per person (US$): 3,590
Principal languages: Polish

ROMANIA
Capital: Bucharest
Area: 237,500 km²
Population: 22,474,000
Currency: Lei
GNP per person (US$): 1,410
Principal languages: Romanian, Magyar, German

SLOVENIA
Capital: Ljubljana
Area: 20,251 km²
Population: 1,993
Currency: Tolar
GNP per person (US$): 9,840
Principal languages: Slovene, Serbo-Croat

SERBIA/MONTENEGRO
Capital: Belgrade
Area: 102,173 km²
Population: 10,635,000
Currency: Lev
GNP per person (US$): 000
Principal languages: Serb

CROATIA
Capital: Zagreb
Area: 56,538 km²
Population: 4,481,000
Currency: Croat Dinar
GNP per person (US$): 4,060
Principal languages: Croat, Serb

BOSNIA-HERZEGOVINA
Capital: Sarajevo
Area: 51,129 km²
Population: 3,675,000
Currency: New Dinar
GNP per person (US$): 2,500
Principal languages: Serbo-Croat

ALBANIA
Capital: Tirana
Area: 28,748 km²
Population: 3,119,000
Currency: Lek
GNP per person (US$): 760
Principal languages: Albanian

MACEDONIA
Capital: Skopje
Area: 25,713 km²
Population: 1,999,000
Currency: Macedonian Dinar
GNP per person (US$): 780
Principal languages: Macedonian, Albanian, Turkish

BULGARIA
Capital: Sofia
Area: 110,912 km²
Population: 8,336,000
Currency: Leva
GNP per person (US$): 1,170
Principal languages: Bulgarian, Turkish

SOUTHERN EUROPE

The countries of southern Europe enjoy mild climates influenced by the Mediterranean Sea and fairly low rainfall. Agriculture is important, including extensive vineyards and olive groves. Tourism is a major source of income, but problems associated with this include pollution and disturbance or destruction of habitats. Turkey is included here, although it differs historically and culturally.

PORTUGAL
Capital: Lisbon
Area: 92,389 km²
Population: 9,869,000
Currency: Escudo
GNP per person (US$): 11,010
Principal languages: Portuguese

ITALY
Capital: Rome
Area: 301,287 km²
Population: 57,369,000
Currency: Italian Lira
GNP per person (US$): 20,170
Principal languages: Italian (German, French, Albanian minorities)

GREECE
Capital: Athens
Area: 131,944 km²
Population: 10,600,000
Currency: Drachma
GNP per person (US$): 11,640
Principal languages: Greek

SPAIN
Capital: Madrid
Area: 504,782 km²
Population: 39,628,000
Currency: Peseta
GNP per person (US$): 14,490
Principal languages: Spanish, Castilian, Catalan, Basque, Galician

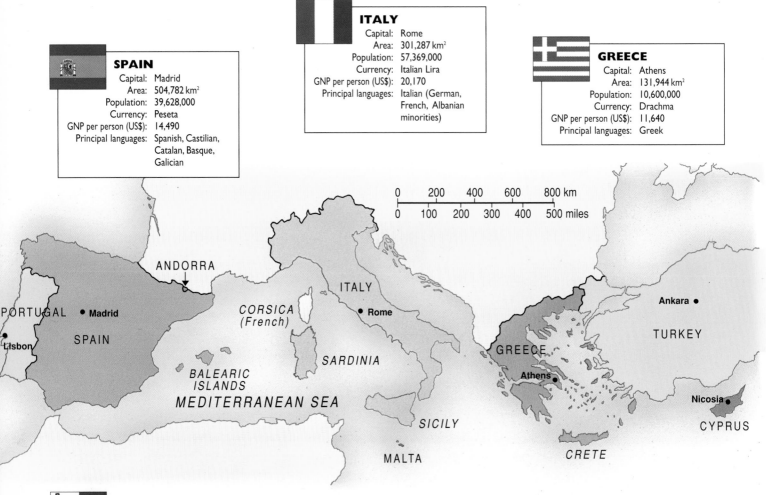

MALTA
Capital: Valetta
Area: 316 km²
Population: 384,000
Currency: Maltese Lira
GNP per person (US$): 9,330
Principal languages: Maltese, English

TURKEY
Capital: Ankara
Area: 779,452 km²
Population: 64,479,000
Currency: Turkish Lira
GNP per person (US$): 3,130
Principal languages: Turkish, Kurdish

CYPRUS
Capital: Nicosia
Area: 9,251 km²
Population: 771,000
Currency: Pound
GNP per person (US$): 10,260
Principal languages: Greek, Turkish

RUSSIAN FEDERATION AND COUNTRIES OF THE FORMER SOVIET UNION

With the collapse of communism in Europe, a number of countries that were formerly part of the Soviet Union claimed independence. Together some formed the Commonwealth of Independent States (CIS). The Russian Federation is still the largest country in the world. These countries have experienced similar changes to the East European countries and are currently adjusting to a free market economy and democratic government.

RUSSIAN FEDERATION
Capital: Moscow
Area: 17,675,400 km²
Population: 147,434,000
Currency: Rouble
GNP per person (US$): 2,680
Principal languages: Russian, Tatar, Ukrainian, Chuvash, Bashkan, Belarussian, Chechen

ESTONIA
Capital: Tallinn
Area: 45,100 km²
Population: 1,429,000
Currency: Krone
GNP per person (US$): 3,360
Principal languages: Estonian, Russian

LATVIA
Capital: Riga
Area: 64,589 km²
Population: 2,242,000
Currency: Lat
GNP per person (US$): 2,430
Principal languages: Lettish, Russian, Belarussian

LITHUANIA
Capital: Vilnius
Area: 65,200 km²
Population: 3,694,000
Currency: Lit
GNP per person (US$): 2,260
Principal languages: Lithuanian, Russian, Polish

BELARUS
Capital: Minsk
Area: 207,600 km²
Population: 10,315,000
Currency: Belarus Rouble
GNP per person (US$): 2,150
Principal languages: Belarussian, Russian, Polish

UKRAINE
Capital: Kiev
Area: 603,700 km²
Population: 50,861,000
Currency: Karbavonet
GNP per person (US$): 1,040
Principal languages: Ukrainian, Russian, Belarussian

GEORGIA
Capital: Tblisi
Area: 69,700 km²
Population: 5,059,000
Currency: Rouble
GNP per person (US$): 860
Principal languages: Georgian, Russian

LAKE ONEGA

LAKE LADOGA

EUROPEAN RUSSIA

Moscow •

0 100 200 300 400 500 600 km
0 100 200 300 400 miles

• Tallinn
ESTONIA

• Riga
LATVIA

LITHUANIA
Vilnius •

• Minsk

BELARUS

• Kiev

UKRAINE

SEA OF AZOV

Tblisi •
GEORGIA

BLACK SEA

INTRODUCTION

Tourists descending into the crater of Mount Vesuvius at Pompeii in Italy.

If we look back at Europe's long history, we see a continent that is constantly changing. There is, perhaps, a greater mixture of cultures and religions in Europe than in any other single continent. In previous centuries, Europe dominated much of the globe. It was the home of the first industrial nations, and the centre of many of the world's scientific discoveries and political systems.

In the twentieth century, Europe has seen two world wars, and in the last ten years there have been further dramatic changes. There has been the collapse of communism in Europe and the splitting up of one of the great 'superpowers' – the Soviet Union or USSR.

There has been the reunification of Germany (the joining of East and West Germany) and the division of other former Eastern European countries, such as Czechoslovakia and Yugoslavia, into smaller states.

THE VIOLENT LAND

Where the Earth's plates meet, lines of weakness or stress often form in its crust and earthquakes or volcanic eruptions can occur. One such fault line runs up through Italy and then turns down through the former Yugoslavia and Greece. Italy is well-known for its volcanoes, Mount Etna and Vesuvius; former Yugoslavia was the scene of many devastating earthquakes. The plates are still moving – nothing can stop them.

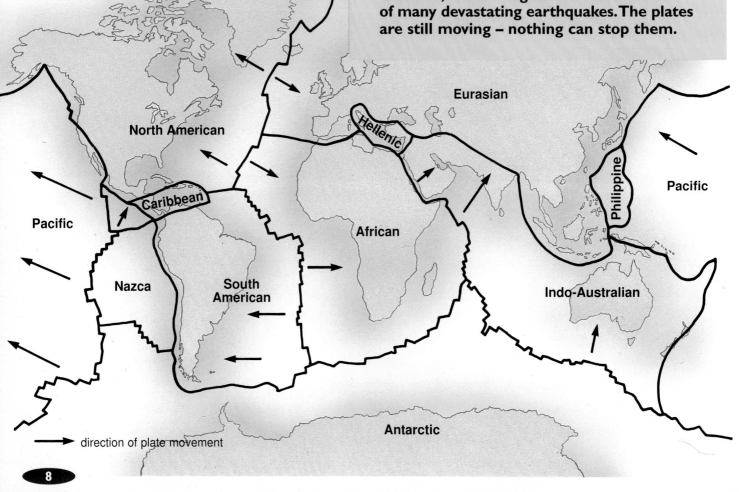

North American

Eurasian

Hellenic

Caribbean

Pacific

Philippine

Pacific

African

Nazca

South American

Indo-Australian

Antarctic

→ direction of plate movement

A WHIRLWIND TOUR

Try to imagine a line that starts somewhere in the frozen wastes of the Arctic Ocean and travels southwards along the gigantic range of mountains called the Urals, across the massive bulk of Russia to a huge inland sea, the Caspian, and finally to the Mediterranean. Everything west of that line we can call Europe.

Now imagine going on a whirlwind tour across this continent. The tour covers arctic ice, vast evergreen forests, fertile plains, great mountain ranges, and warm, dry hills clad in olive groves. We encounter different peoples, a bewildering variety of languages, stunning buildings and fantastic technology. We see great wealth, wars and grinding poverty. We have caught a glimpse of Europe.

THE MAKING OF A CONTINENT

It is impossible to say exactly when Europe was formed. All continents were created by the gradual movement of huge, rocky plates drifting on the earth's semi-molten mantle (outer layer). As the plates crashed together, mountain ranges such as the Grampians in Scotland and the Urals in Russia were pushed up. Then, about 150 million years ago, the American continents tore away from Europe and Africa, and the great Atlantic Ocean was formed. Between Africa and Europe, part of this new sea poured into a lowland and so the Mediterranean was born.

This process, called continental drift, is just one of the forces that have created the Europe we recognize today. Other forces have also shaped and moulded the land. Rivers have carved out great valleys and plains; wind and rain have worn away mountain ranges; ice and frost have split and shattered rocks. And from north to central Europe, the unstoppable movement of great glaciers has drilled and gouged out the face of the land.

This book is about some of the forces, both physical and human, which have made Europe what it is today. Perhaps it may also give some clues to how this changing continent may develop in the future.

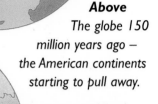

Above
The globe 150 million years ago – the American continents starting to pull away.

Left *The globe 50 million years ago.*

Below *A satellite photo of the globe today with a view of Europe.*

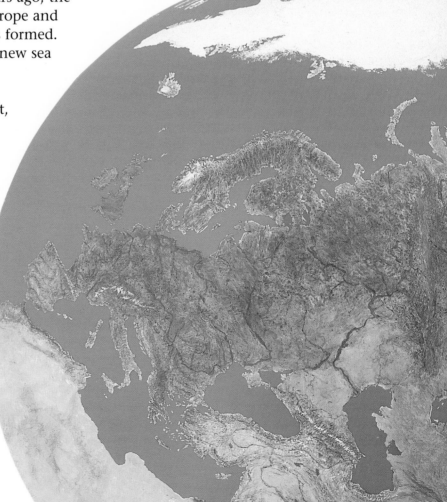

THE GEOGRAPHY OF EUROPE

Europe ranks sixth in size among the continents, covering a total of 10,531,623 km². Only Australia is smaller. Europe is made up of more than forty countries, some of which have the most densely populated land areas in the world. The total population is over 665 million – an average of sixty-three people per km². To understand Europe, we must look beyond the borders of individual countries. We must look at Europe as a whole.

Benidorm is one of Spain's busiest holiday resorts. Much of Europe's coastline is naturally very beautiful, and the creation of high-rise holiday complexes such as this has been criticized for spoiling the coasts.

BESIDE THE SEA

The seas and oceans have always played an important part in Europe's history and development. They speeded early exploration and trade; they have yielded a rich harvest of fish; more recently, they have become a source of energy as natural gas and oil (petroleum) were discovered in the North Sea.

Water surrounds Europe on three sides: in the north the Barents Sea borders the icy coastline of northern Russia and Finland; along the western flank the North Sea and Atlantic Ocean pound Europe's shores; in the south, the coast is lapped by the warm waters of the Mediterranean Sea.

The Mediterranean is the world's largest inland sea. Its length is over 4,000 km and its area 2,965,500 km². In some parts it reaches the incredible depth of 5,000 m! The waters of the Mediterranean are more salty than the Atlantic Ocean, which it joins through the narrow Straits of Gibraltar. The warm, steady climate, excellent harbours, and the gently sloping, fertile land that surrounds the Mediterranean, encouraged early civilizations to develop round its shores. Now it is Europe's most popular tourist area.

Two other great inland seas, the Baltic and the Black Sea, influence Europe. The Black Sea is as big as Sweden and reaches a depth of 2,210 m. It remains free of ice all year round, making it important, both economically and strategically, for the countries of the former Soviet Union. Its saltiness is only about half that of seawater and even less where great rivers such as the Danube and Volga flow into it.

The Baltic is really an arm of the Atlantic Ocean, connected to it by two narrow passages, the Kattegat and Skagerrak. It is similar in size to the Black Sea, but much shallower and even less salty. Like the Mediterranean, the Baltic is easily polluted, because waste from the ageing industries of Eastern Europe pours into it and the relatively small volume of water doesn't disperse the pollution as easily as a larger ocean would. About a third of the sea now supports no life at all.

MEDITERRANEAN UNDER THREAT

Carlo Ambretti runs a diving school in Palermo, Sicily. Beneath the water's surface, he sees evidence of pollution all around. Most comes from human and industrial waste and the transportation of oil. He sees marine life, especially sponges and coral, being damaged and beaches being closed to tourists. The region, including his diving business, suffers. He knows that the solution is tighter controls on industry and on the new hotels that spring up like mushrooms along the coast. But he also knows that many of the Mediterranean countries will delay in order to protect their own interests. He sometimes despairs that effective action will ever be taken.

Yalta, Ukraine, is a popular tourist resort on the Black Sea.

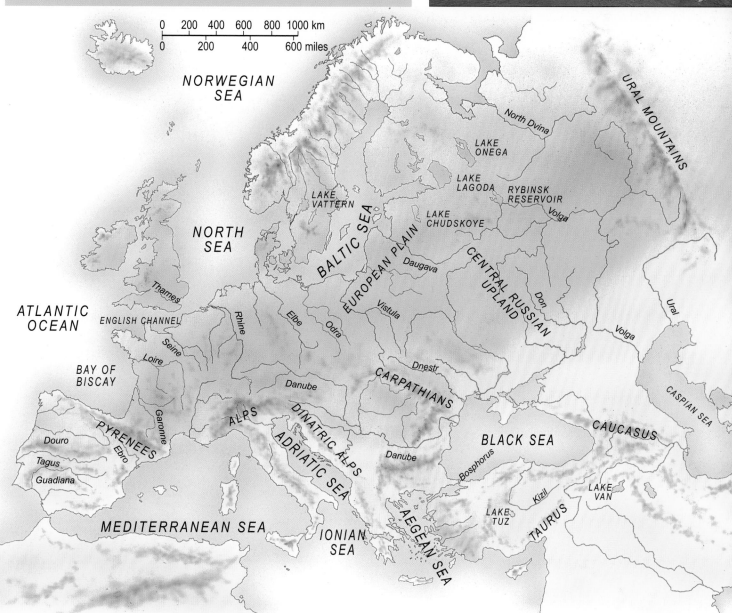

MOUNTAINS AND MORAINES

We can divide the physical map of Europe into two main areas. The west and southern portions are made up of a complicated pattern of mountains, valleys, high plateaus and lowlands. In contrast, eastern Europe consists of a more uniform platform of old, hard rock giving rise to flatter, less spectacular landscapes.

Set against this basic structure are the effects of ice and weathering. The northern third of the continent was altered by glaciation from about 2 million to 10,000 years ago. The hard, ancient mountains of Scotland and Scandinavia were rounded by the scouring (wearing away) action of moving ice, while debris or moraine (material carried by the glaciers) was deposited in the valleys. Melting ice filled many lakes in northern Europe, including the Baltic Sea. The deep fiords of Norway were formed by the action of glaciers on river valleys.

Left Like their northern counterparts, the high mountains of the south – the Alps, the Pyrenees and the Caucasus – have been affected by glaciers which deepen the valleys and sharpen the peaks. This glacier of Pre de Bar is in the Italian Alps.

Below Glaciers grind deep valleys out of mountains, and the melting ice, lower down, forms rivers and lakes.

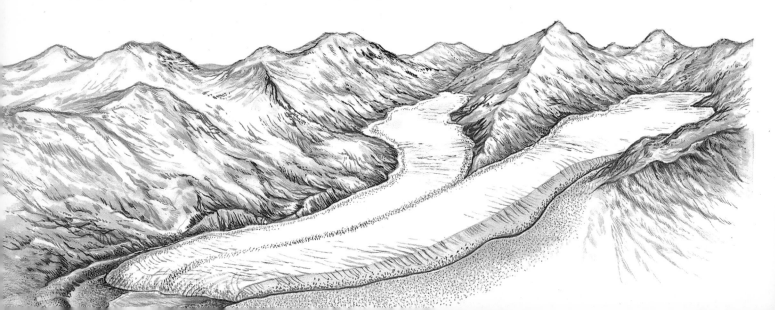

The great mountain ranges of Europe were formed at different times, but all were created by the slow, unstoppable movement of the earth's crust. The north-west highlands of Scandinavia and Scotland, and the eastern Urals, were formed over 200 million years ago. So, too, was the *Massif Central* of France – ancient mountains worn down and then uplifted again to form high plateaus. The Alps, Pyrenees, Carpathians and the Sierra Nevada of southern Spain are mere youngsters by comparison, perhaps less than 10 million years old!

Much of Europe is low-lying. At the far eastern edge of the continent, the surface of the Caspian Sea is 28 m below sea level. Denmark's highest point is less than 175 m. Central Europe and much of western Europe have lowland plains, made fertile by material left by the retreating ice and the flooding of river valleys.

Parts of southern Europe, such as Italy, former Yugoslavia, Turkey and Greece, are subject to volcanic eruptions and violent earthquakes as a result of movement in the earth's crust. Sometimes it is possible to predict eruptions or 'quakes', but predictions are often imprecise, and the size and exact location of the disturbance unknown. Sometimes they are completely unexpected.

Above *Thirty per cent of the land in The Netherlands lies below sea level. Storm surge barriers like this one at Roompot help to prevent flooding.*

EARTHQUAKE!

In 1988 in Armenia, Russia, an earthquake killed 60,000 people. One survivor said, 'The earthquake came without warning three nights ago. We had no chance to get out. The flats collapsed like a pack of cards. We are angry because the expensive flats on the hill have remained intact. Our block was built on mud and rotten concrete!'

On 21 August 1999, an earthquake measuring 7.4 on the Richter scale hit the town of Izmit in Turkey. The earthquake was the worst in Turkey in over 50 years and over 6,000 people died as hundreds of apartment blocks collapsed. The death toll was higher than it should have been because many of the apartment blocks were built recently using cheap, flimsy materials.

THE WEATHER

Europe experiences practically every kind of climate: there are places that hardly ever rise above freezing, and places that are hot and dry most of the year round.

The west of the continent has a maritime climate. This means that it is affected by wet westerly winds coming from the Atlantic. Temperatures are moderate (neither very hot nor cold). At La Coruña in north-western Spain temperatures average 18 °C in July and 10 °C in January. Colder winters occur further north, for example in the UK and Norway. But, even there, their severity is reduced by the Gulf Stream, a current of warm water that flows from the Gulf of Mexico. Rain and snow fall evenly, usually between 510–1,015 mm per year.

The continental climate of central and eastern Europe has much harsher winters and cooler summers. In Moscow, temperatures average -12 °C in January and 16 °C in July and annual precipitation (rain and snow) averages 635 mm. Most occurs in the summer, when there are violent storms as rising air, heated by the land, cools and sheds its moisture.

PRESSURE SYSTEMS

Europe's climate is affected by air pressure systems. Areas of low pressure, developing over Iceland, cause the frequently changing weather patterns experienced by northern and western Europe. Areas of high pressure develop over southern Europe during the summer, causing hot, dry, stable weather. Meanwhile, low pressure over eastern Europe and Asia pulls moist air from the Atlantic into central Europe, giving rainy summers. Finally, high pressure over Siberia in the winter pushes cold, dry air over into eastern and central Europe, accounting for their chilly winters.

Norway is a mountainous country with a long coastline. The sea goes deep into the country, in the form of fiords such as this one. Norway's climate is affected by the sea's closeness.

The regions of the Mediterranean, warmed by the sea, have dry, hot summers (22 °C in July) and mild, rainy winters (8 °C in January). Rainfall averages about 760 mm, but rises to over 1,000 mm on high ground.

Finally, mountain areas have a wide range of climatic conditions depending on their height and the direction of the prevailing (most common) winds. Temperatures range from well below freezing to 16 °C and precipitation ranges from 510 mm in the hills to more than 2,000 mm on the peaks.

VEGETATION

Climate, terrain and soil all affect the natural vegetation found in different parts of Europe. The far north of Scandinavia and Russia is known as the tundra region: moss, lichen and dwarf birch grow in the thin, permanently wet, acid soil. To the south is a broad zone of coniferous trees, the taiga, growing on poor, grey soil. Further south still, across most of western and central Europe, the richer soil and warmer climate support deciduous forest – mainly oak and beech, although much has now been cleared for timber and agriculture. As we move into the Mediterranean region, the natural vegetation becomes more drought-resistant – maquis, cypress, cork oak, low scrubby evergreens and olives. Because there is low rainfall, decay is slow and the soil is poor in humus (organic matter).

In eastern Europe and Russia, coniferous and deciduous forest gives way to high, flat plains, either wooded or more commonly covered in vast areas of prairie grass (steppe). These areas are the most fertile in Europe, but the unpredictable rainfall and the poor climate mean that agricultural production often suffers. Steppe is replaced further south by drought-resistant vegetation or even desert.

- Alpine and tundra
- Mountain vegetation
- Coniferous forest
- Deciduous forest
- Mixed forest
- Grassland
- Mediterranean
- Scrub and semidesert

THE HISTORY OF EUROPE

The history of Europe is all about change. Even great empires, such as those of the Greeks and Romans, were constantly changing, moulded by forces both from within and from outside. Sometimes, changes occurred as a result of new ideas or ways of understanding the world. Many, however, were the result of different nations or religions seeking to expand their influence. Often countries formed alliances with other countries to strengthen their own position. These alliances also changed over time.

It would be easy to think that most of the countries of Europe were constantly at war with each other, or that life was always hard. But the history of Europe is also one of the development of science and art, and the gradual improvement of human conditions and quality of life.

THE QUEST FOR RESOURCES

One of the factors that speeded up the development of Europe was the search for new land and resources. In the fifteenth and sixteenth centuries, Portuguese sailors began searching for a sea route to India

Below The exploration and trade routes of the fifteenth and sixteenth centuries. By then, European traders had spread across much of the world, including Africa and Asia.

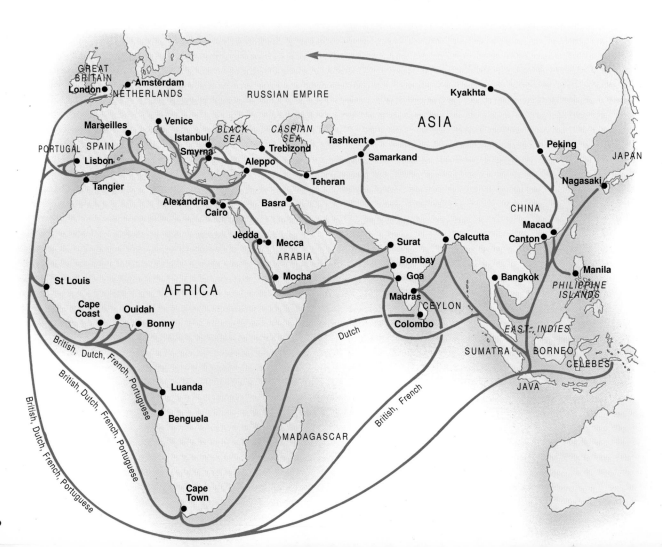

to gain access to the valuable spice trade of the East. In 1498, Vasco da Gama sailed into the Indian Ocean. Six years earlier, Christopher Columbus had discovered the West Indies, and further Spanish and Portuguese expeditions reached the South American mainland. Often, the arrival of Europeans spelled disaster for the indigenous (native) people and their culture. The empires of the Aztecs and Incas in South America were conquered and then destroyed by the Spanish, their cities devastated and their treasures looted. Many Indians were killed in fighting, forced into slavery or died of European diseases.

Above *Sailing clippers like the Cutty Sark carried tea and other goods for the East India Company, a group of London merchants who traded in the East. The Cutty Sark is now berthed at Greenwich, London.*

COLONIALISM

In the seventeenth century, British, Dutch and French trading companies, spurred on by rivalry between the nations, set up trading posts and colonies in Africa, India and the Far East (East Asia). North America also attracted British settlers, in search of land or freedom from religious persecution, but who went on to destroy many Native American towns and settlements. Other colonies were developed for growing sugar, cotton and tobacco, using slaves captured and sent from West Africa. By the mid-eighteenth century most of India was under British control and, at the beginning of the nineteenth century, almost the entire continent of Africa was colonized by European powers.

Below *The European colonies in Africa, India and the Far East (East Asia) at the end of the nineteenth century.*

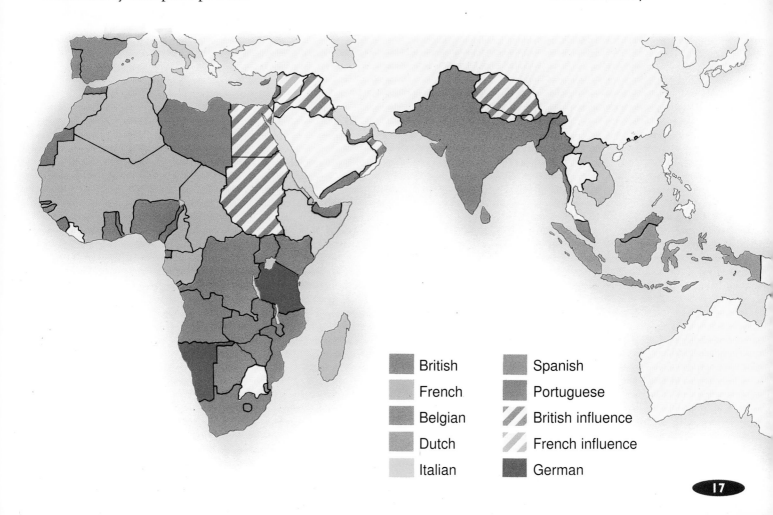

■ British	■ Spanish
■ French	■ Portuguese
■ Belgian	▨ British influence
■ Dutch	▨ French influence
■ Italian	■ German

EUROPE AT WAR

In 1914, there was a delicate balance between two major powers in Europe: Germany and Austria-Hungary on one hand and France, Russia and Britain on the other. The assassination of the heir to the Austrian throne triggered a European war – the First World War – that was to see some of the most horrific battles in history. Germany and its allies finally surrendered in 1918, but the terms of the surrender were harsh. As the German people became more and more discontented with living conditions after the war, Adolf Hitler skilfully turned this to his advantage. By 1933, his Nazi Party had absolute control of Germany and any opposition was crushed ruthlessly. In 1939, Hitler's armies took over part of former Czechoslavakia (now the Czech Republic), where many Germans lived. On 1 September 1939, Germany invaded Poland. Britain and her allies could no longer ignore this threat and two days later, on 3 September 1939, the Second World War began.

Using a series of lightning attacks (*Blitzkrieg*), Germany rapidly conquered Norway, Denmark, Belgium, the Netherlands and Luxembourg. By June 1940, France was occupied. Britain was the target of massive bombing raids but the victory of the Royal Air Force over the German *Luftwaffe* persuaded Hitler not to attempt an invasion. The focus of the war shifted to the Mediterranean and the Balkans, where Germany's ally – Italy – was also fighting. In June 1941, Hitler attacked Russia but the harshness of the Russian winter and the vast Soviet army checked his advance.

This picture was taken on 2 November 1940 from St. Paul's Cathedral, London. It shows the devastation to churches, historic buildings and office buildings caused by the 'sea of fire' – the intense German fire bombing raids.

Main picture *A turning point in the Second World War was the Japanese attack on Pearl Harbour on 7 December 1941. This is the explosion of the USS Shaw during the attack.*
Inset *US Assault Troops in a landing craft approach the northern coast of France during the D Day landings.*

By 1942, the tide of the war began to change. Japan had signed a pact with Germany and Italy. Its attack on the US fleet anchored in Pearl Habour, Hawaii, had brought the USA into the war. There were important victories for the allies at El Alamein in North Africa and at Stalingrad in Russia. In May 1944, the German lines in Italy were broken. On 6 June 1944, D Day, the allies launched a re-invasion of Europe under the code name Operation Overlord. In April 1945, Russian and allied troops, fighting from opposite directions, met in Berlin. Germany was defeated and surrendered on 8 May 1945. The most costly European war of all time had ended.

THE FALL OF COLONIALISM

The effects of the Second World War were widespread. Between 1947 and 1975, the entire colonial system of Europe disintegrated. Weakened by the war, countries like Britain and the Netherlands could no longer sustain their overseas empires. The colonies themselves demanded freedom from foreign interference and occupation. Often the colonial powers left peacefully, but in areas such as Southeast Asia there was bitter fighting. Independence was frequently followed by civil wars to decide who should govern. New, democratically elected governments were overthrown by military dictatorships. European countries had stripped away much of the wealth and even culture of their former colonies and left them poorly equipped to develop on their own.

THE RISE AND FALL OF THE IRON CURTAIN

Western bloc
Eastern bloc
Iron Curtain

The Iron Curtain divided Eastern and Western Bloc countries for almost forty years, from the 1950s to the 1980s.

1989 saw the destruction of the Wall that divided Berlin. Soon afterwards East and West Germany were united.

At the end of the Second World War, Soviet forces occupied much of eastern Europe and other allied forces occupied the west. As the rebuilding of Europe began, it split along political or ideological lines. This 'new Europe' was divided sharply between the communist East and the non-communist West. The line dividing Eastern Europe and the Soviet Union (the Eastern Bloc) from Western Europe and the USA (the Western Bloc) became known as the Iron Curtain. There was a permanent state of hostility between the two blocs, called the Cold War. Actual fighting did not occur, partly perhaps because of the huge arsenals of nuclear weapons owned by both sides which, had they been used, would have obliterated everyone.

The two halves of Europe developed very differently. In the West, US aid, new technology, increasing integration between countries, and the rapid rebuilding of West Germany's shattered industries, led to swift economic recovery. At first Eastern Europe and the USSR, although devastated by the war, also recovered rapidly. But increasing centralization and state control led to inefficiency and stagnation. Many of these countries were plagued by oppression (lack of individual freedom) and poverty. These conditions led to people's uprisings which were ruthlessly put down by the Soviet Union. The unrest continued, however, and in 1987, the Soviet leader, Mikhail Gorbachev, made it clear that the satellite states (including Poland, Hungary, Czechoslavakia, East Germany, Bulgaria and Albania) could choose their own form of government. By 1991, elections had been held in every country in the region, including the Soviet Union, which had itself begun to dissolve into individual countries. Some of these countries, such as Belarus and the Russian Federation itself, formed themselves into a new alliance called the Commonwealth of Independent States (CIS). Others, such as Estonia, Lithuania and Latvia (the Baltic States) and the Ukraine looked towards Western Europe and the European Union for their future.

A NEW CONFLICT

Freed from the Soviet system, the countries of Eastern Europe encountered new problems. The change to a Western economy was not easy for countries that were already poor. Some were uneasy about embracing 'Western values' and tried to slow down the rate of change. More damaging still was the speed with which old nationalist and ethnic feelings returned. Nowhere was this more marked than in Yugoslavia. Abandoning communism in 1991, the country simply fell apart, reviving ethnic differences going back many hundreds of years.

WHERE EAST MEETS WEST

To simply suggest that Western Europe 'had it right' and Eastern Europe 'had it wrong' would be a serious mis-statement. The Eastern countries had always been poorer than the Western ones. The communist states provided free education and healthcare, there was full employment and housing was available (if not of high standard). There were ideals of fairness and equality from which other political and social systems could learn. A 'Western' way of life can bring many of its own problems, such as high crime rates and an increasing gap between rich and poor. Some of these problems are now occurring in the former communist countries as well as in the West.

The two great religious cultures of East and West, Islam and Christianity, have also dominated much of Europe's history and development. Despite so-called 'religious' conflicts, such as the Crusades and the war in Bosnia, such differences have enriched European culture and thinking over the centuries. The new Europe has to learn how to live with all these differences and benefit from the variety of ideas, beliefs and ways of life that they bring.

The Soviet leader, Mikhail Gorbachev, visiting Berlin, East Germany. Gorbachev's relaxation of hard-line communism inside the Soviet Union was the starting point for the collapse of communism in Eastern Europe.

THE PEOPLES OF EUROPE

The peoples of Europe have been constantly on the move, bringing new ideas and cultures with them. One result of this has been the large number of small countries and principalities that exist in Europe today, based on ethnic, language, cultural or religious differences.

Some people move from country to country to find better living conditions (economic migrants). Movements may be within Europe or from outside, for example the (often illegal) flow of people from North Africa into Italy and Spain. Other migrations are the result of injustice.

GREAT AND TERRIBLE JOURNEYS

The mass movement of people, or migration, has always been part of European history. As early as the fifteenth century, Jews were expelled from Spain as Christian influences moved south. Often such journeys were to escape religious or political persecution. Following the end of the First World War, new frontiers were drawn up that left different ethnic groups scattered throughout eastern Europe. The effect was a massive movement of people throughout the continent, fleeing new rulers, communism or the newly emerging Fascist regimes in Italy, Spain and Germany.

Those fleeing persecution from Nazi Germany in the 1930s were mainly Jews, who were blamed, quite unjustly, for Germany's economic difficulties. At first, they were encouraged to leave, but this was soon followed by internment (imprisonment) and then extermination (mass murder) in an attempt by the Nazis to eliminate all but a 'pure race'. Many Jews endured journeys of extreme danger, knowing they would be killed if they were discovered. Often they were children, smuggled out of the country by friends or relatives, leaving their parents behind. By 1939, there was no further escape; millions of Jews in Germany and Poland perished in Nazi concentration camps. The worst episode in European history had begun.

Above As Christianity is the principal religion of Europe, Jews have often suffered for their beliefs. Here a boy at his Barmitzvah reads from the Torah.

Below The main twentieth century European migrations.

After the Second World War, the collapse of Germany released millions of prisoners-of-war and 'slave-workers' to return home; some 5 million Russian prisoners, refugees and servicemen were sent back to Russia, many against their will, to face an uncertain future. Millions of Germans were expelled from Germany's pre-war territories and from the lands they had annexed (taken over) in 1939. Further movement resulted from the westward expansion of the Soviet Union into countries such as Estonia and Latvia.

In 1991, the break-up of Yugoslavia resulted in bitter conflict between different ethnic groups. One feature of the conflict has been so-called 'ethnic cleansing' – the forced movement of people from their homes in an attempt to create 'racially pure' areas. Hundreds of thousands of refugees were driven into concentration camps or forced to 'return' to their country of ethnic origin.

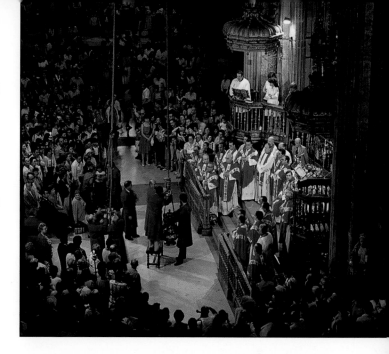

In southern European countries the majority of people are Catholics. This is a pilgrims' mass at the Cathedral of Santiago de Compostela in Spain.

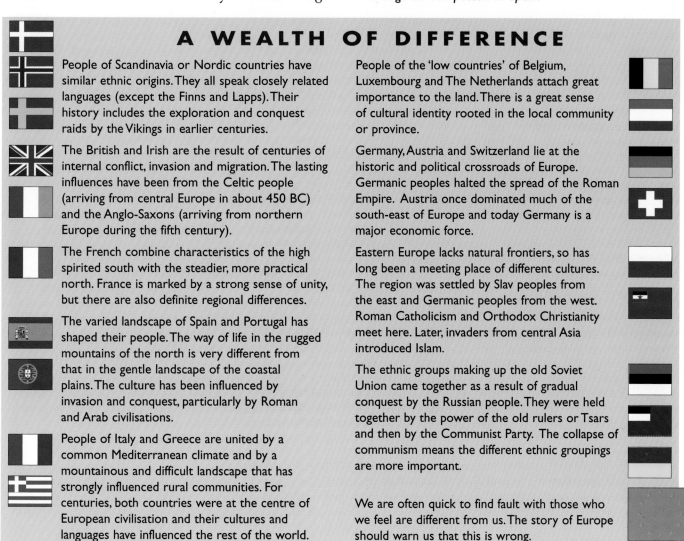

A WEALTH OF DIFFERENCE

People of Scandinavia or Nordic countries have similar ethnic origins. They all speak closely related languages (except the Finns and Lapps). Their history includes the exploration and conquest raids by the Vikings in earlier centuries.

The British and Irish are the result of centuries of internal conflict, invasion and migration. The lasting influences have been from the Celtic people (arriving from central Europe in about 450 BC) and the Anglo-Saxons (arriving from northern Europe during the fifth century).

The French combine characteristics of the high spirited south with the steadier, more practical north. France is marked by a strong sense of unity, but there are also definite regional differences.

The varied landscape of Spain and Portugal has shaped their people. The way of life in the rugged mountains of the north is very different from that in the gentle landscape of the coastal plains. The culture has been influenced by invasion and conquest, particularly by Roman and Arab civilisations.

People of Italy and Greece are united by a common Mediterranean climate and by a mountainous and difficult landscape that has strongly influenced rural communities. For centuries, both countries were at the centre of European civilisation and their cultures and languages have influenced the rest of the world.

People of the 'low countries' of Belgium, Luxembourg and The Netherlands attach great importance to the land. There is a great sense of cultural identity rooted in the local community or province.

Germany, Austria and Switzerland lie at the historic and political crossroads of Europe. Germanic peoples halted the spread of the Roman Empire. Austria once dominated much of the south-east of Europe and today Germany is a major economic force.

Eastern Europe lacks natural frontiers, so has long been a meeting place of different cultures. The region was settled by Slav peoples from the east and Germanic peoples from the west. Roman Catholicism and Orthodox Christianity meet here. Later, invaders from central Asia introduced Islam.

The ethnic groups making up the old Soviet Union came together as a result of gradual conquest by the Russian people. They were held together by the power of the old rulers or Tsars and then by the Communist Party. The collapse of communism means the different ethnic groupings are more important.

We are often quick to find fault with those who we feel are different from us. The story of Europe should warn us that this is wrong.

LIVING IN EUROPE TODAY

Europe is one of the most densely-populated and urbanized parts of the world. Even in rural countries, in southern Europe and parts of eastern Europe, people tend to be clustered around villages and small towns. Population densities are greatest in the highly industrialized areas of western Europe. More than 60 per cent of the population of Europe is classified as urban, with the highest proportion (95 per cent) in Belgium.

In general, most Europeans enjoy a reasonable standard of living, are well-educated and have access to healthcare. Working conditions, particularly in the countries of the European Union (EU), are generally good. A trend in employment throughout Europe in recent years has been the expansion of part-time and temporary work, sometimes at the expense of full-time or more secure employment. Although women now enjoy equality with men in most areas of economic and social life, unfair differences still exist. Women and young people under 25 are more likely to be affected by unemployment.

These statements conceal many differences between countries, regions, and urban and rural areas. The countries of northern Europe, which are more industrialized and better-equipped with infrastructure (transport and communication networks and other services like hospitals), generally have a higher standard of living than those in the south. Rural areas tend to be poorer than urban areas, although there are increasing numbers of badly supported inner city areas, where jobs, housing, recreational opportunities and good education are sometimes impossible to find. The difference between levels of wealth in Western and Eastern European countries is also still very marked.

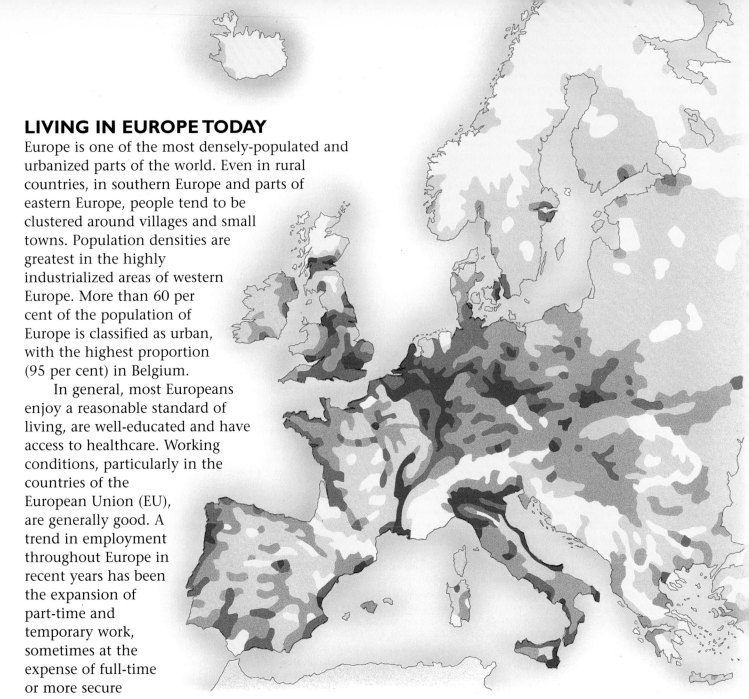

Europe's population densities.

Per mile²	Per km²
Over 500	Over 200
250–500	100–200
100–250	40–100
25–100	10–40
0–25	0–10

HEALTHCARE

Although levels of healthcare are reasonable in much of Europe, there is a strong relationship between poverty and poor health. Healthcare is increasingly aimed at preventive measures, such as the promotion of healthier life-styles, better diet and increased exercise. Death rates have fallen in the last 20 years, but deaths due to cancer and heart and circulatory disease are still high. The loss of life due to road accidents, particularly among young people, is especially bad. Each year, in the EU alone, 45,000 people are killed on roads and over 1.5 million injured. The vast majority of these accidents are preventable, and this would reduce all deaths of people aged 15–24 by over a third!

CARDBOARD CITY

Margaret lives in a cardboard box in one of Europe's wealthiest cities. Once she had a home, a job and a family. When her factory closed, she could no longer keep up her rent and she was evicted from her small flat. Unable to cope, her children were taken into care. With no income and nowhere to live, she travelled to London to look for work. But London was worse. The hostels were overcrowded and unsafe. Soon she was sleeping rough with others outside Waterloo Station, using cardboard boxes for warmth. Now she survives on hand-outs from commuters who can't understand how such a situation can arise in a wealthy country.

Economic changes in Poland have caused severe unemployment. This man begs in the streets of Warsaw.

EDUCATION

All European countries take the education of young people seriously. All children of primary age attend school full time. At secondary level, there are some differences, partly related to school leaving age. In Italy and Portugal, for example, children can leave school at 14, this rises to 15 in Greece, Ireland and Luxembourg and 16 in Denmark and the UK. In some countries, such as Germany and Belgium, all young people are required to continue some form of part-time training or education until 18. Boys and girls are generally equally represented at all levels of education.

About 30 per cent of young people in Europe take part in some form of higher or further education or training. These are French students of engineering.

The Tour de France is an international cycling event watched by over a third of the French population.

The European Union (EU) runs projects to encourage educational links with other countries, including Eastern Europe. 'Lingua' is a programme designed to improve the teaching of foreign languages. 'Youth for Europe' is another scheme to support the exchange of young people outside the school system. There are also a number of European Schools, providing an international syllabus and enabling students to gain admission to universities throughout the EU.

LEISURE AND FOOD

Europeans have a wide range of leisure interests. Many Scandinavians own country cabins in the mountains or forests or on the coast. Membership of sports clubs is very high and skiing and other winter sports are extremely popular. Satellite and cable broadcasting has brought many new programmes to Scandinavia.

The French are well-known for their love of good food and each region has its own distinctive style. France is also well-known for its stylish clothes and Paris is a world centre for fashion.

The people of the lowland countries, particularly the Netherlands, place great importance on their relationships. This allows a high degree of personal freedom, set within an ordered way of life. Tradition and art are both important. Football plays a significant part in the lives of many people in the Netherlands and clubs like PSV Eindhoven and Ajax Amsterdam have international reputations.

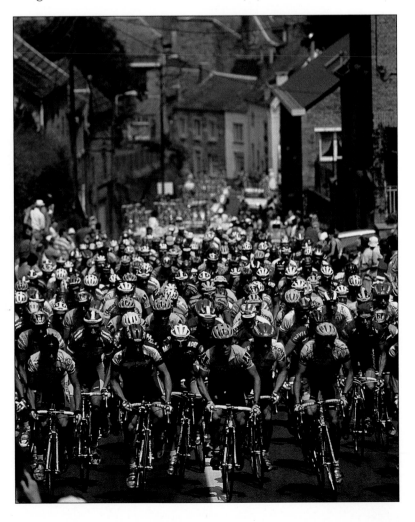

Home-based activities such as gardening, watching television and home improvements are popular leisure pursuits for people in the UK. Equally popular are watching or playing team games such as soccer, rugby and cricket. Many Britons are interested in the history and heritage of the country. The National Trust, which preserves historic buildings and landscapes, has over 1 million members.

Years of occupation by Arab civilisations have left a strong mark on eating habits in the south of Spain. Paella (chicken and seafood cooked with spiced rice) resembles the dishes of North Africa and the Middle East. Football is now the national sporting pastime in Spain. Folk song, music and dance are very much part of national and regional identity.

Both Greece and Italy place great value on traditional society. In some areas of southern Italy and in the mountainous regions and islands of Greece, the old customs of the Mediterranean village are still be to found. Pride in towns is very strong, often shown in rivalry between football teams such as Inter Milan and Juventus of Turin. Italian food is now a common sight in restaurants throughout the world. Italian cinema is also admired worldwide for its variety and creativity.

The countries of central Europe, such as Germany, Switzerland and Austria, have a rich variety of food and take pleasure in the social activities of eating and drinking. Austria is famous for its cafes and food, wine and beer festivals are common in Germany. Switzerland has its dairy products, especially cheeses and chocolate. Many German cities also have internationally famous opera houses, ballet companies and museums. The Salzburg Festival in Austria stages some of the most spectacular operas in the world.

A bullfight in southern Spain. Bullfighting is still popular in southern Spain, but there is a move towards the Portuguese form of fighting, which spares the bull's life (but which many still condemn as unnecessarily cruel).

The effect of communism, when religious and ethnic differences were suppressed, has had a marked influence on the countries of Eastern Europe and the Balkans. Since 1989, these differences have again emerged, resulting both in conflict and in an enriching of local cultures and activities. Now Eastern Europe is coping with an influx of Western ideas and values. Foreign goods fill the shops and advertisements for new products fill the streets. Some differences were never lost. Hungarians had kept their preference for paprika, goulash and strudel. Sauerkraut and kielbasa sausage were favoured by Poles. Czechoslovaks drank strong beers, Poles vodka and Hungarians fine wines.

WORKING TOGETHER: EUROPEAN CO-OPERATION

The terrible destruction and loss of life in the Second World War acted as a spur for greater co-operation between the countries of Western Europe. The Organization for Economic Co-operation and Development (now the OECD), formed in 1948, was the first joint body to enable European countries to work together.

THE EUROPEAN UNION (EU)

In 1951, six countries – France, Italy, West Germany, Belgium, Luxembourg and the Netherlands – signed the Treaty of Paris to create a common market in coal and steel. For the first time, this new community had powers that crossed national boundaries. These countries then launched the idea of economic co-operation over all goods. In 1957, the Treaty of Rome was signed, establishing the European Economic Community (EEC) or Common Market. The ultimate aim was an ever-closer union among the peoples of Europe, but the first task was to allow greater freedom of movement of people, goods, services and capital (money) across the borders of the member states.

Gradually, the EEC expanded to include more nations. By 1995, there were fifteen members of the Community, the most recent being Sweden and Finland. Soon there will be more. To mark the move to greater integration between these countries, the EEC is now known as the European Union or EU.

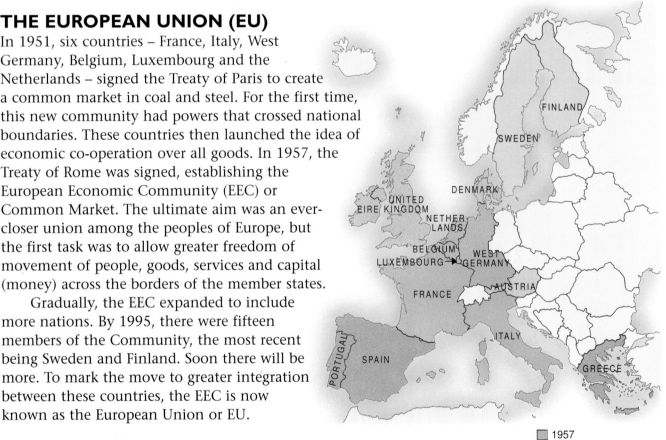

- ☐ 1957
- ☐ 1973
- ☐ 1981
- ☐ 1986
- ☐ 1995

The fifteen EU countries with dates of joining – France, Italy, West Germany, Belgium, Luxembourg and the Netherlands (1957); UK, Eire and Denmark (1973); Greece (1981); Portugal and Spain (1986), Austria, Sweden and Finland (1995).

STRAIGHT CUCUMBERS AND REGULATION APPLES ONLY, PLEASE!

Some people are concerned that European regulations can be too petty and that, eventually, everything we buy or do will be regulated by 'Brussels'. In fact, most legislation is designed to improve people's living and working conditions, and to create fairer practices, for example in relation to employment. Sometimes there do seem to be examples of over-regulation, although there has never been a ban on curved cucumbers, as some English newspapers claimed!

The EU is run by a number of decision-making and administrative bodies.

THE EUROPEAN PARLIAMENT

This is made up of elected members (MEPs) from the member states who meet in Strasbourg for a week each month. The Parliament agrees the EU's budget and has some powers over its policies. Its powers are much more limited, however, than those of national parliaments.

THE COUNCIL OF MINISTERS

The real power lies in the hands of the Council of Ministers, which is made up of representatives of the governments of the member states. Usually these are the foreign ministers, but this will depend on the topic being discussed. Twice a year, the heads of states themselves (eg. Britain's Prime Minister and France's President) meet. All major decisions concerning the EU are made by the Council.

THE EUROPEAN COMMISSION

The administration of the EU is carried out by the European Commission from Brussels. It is run by a number of offices led by Commissioners from different member states. Each has responsibility for an area of the EU's work such as agriculture, environment or transport.

THE EUROPEAN COURT OF JUSTICE

The Court of Justice, based in Luxembourg, is the supreme legal body of the EU: its judgements have to be obeyed by national courts and countries in matters relating to Community affairs. Anyone, from individuals to member states, can bring appeals against the Community's laws to the Court, if they think they are unfair.

THE EUROPEAN INVESTMENT BANK

This finances major projects in order to encourage the balanced development of the Community. A Court of Auditors checks the Community's spending.

The flags of member countries hang outside the European Parliament building in Strasbourg.

COUNCIL FOR MUTUAL ECONOMIC ASSISTANCE (CMEA)

In 1949, the countries of Eastern Europe formed their own economic union called the Council for Mutual Economic Assistance (CMEA). This was designed to share resources and help development of the member states. With the collapse of communism in 1989, the CMEA also collapsed and individual countries began to increase their trade with the West. One result has been that trade between the former CMEA countries has fallen dramatically. These difficulties will need to be addressed if Eastern Europe countries and the Commonwealth of Independent States (CIS) are to take their place among the successful economies of Europe.

A LAND OF RESOURCES

Europe is a continent of great natural resources. It is also a great industrial and manufacturing community. The countries of the EU alone accounted for 31 per cent of all world exported goods in 1993, compared to 23.7 per cent for the US and 18.2 per cent for Japan.

But Europe is also a high consuming continent; the majority of its people enjoy – and expect – a high standard of living. Europe uses up its own (and others) resources rapidly; some would say, wastefully. Its consumption of energy is huge, while much of Eastern Europe's industry still lags far behind the rest of the continent in its efficiency and environmental performance.

BUILDING ON COAL AND STEEL

Europe has been well-supplied with two basic commodities that have allowed it to develop into a highly industrialized society – coal and iron ore. Coal deposits are widespread throughout Europe with the exception of Scandinavia and the Mediterranean countries. In 1990, Europe produced one-fifth of the world's anthracite and bituminous coal. Europe now only produces one-fiftieth of the world output of iron ore, but is still a major producer of steel, from imported ore.

Other important minerals are bauxite (aluminium ore) and potash (used in fertilizers and chemical processes). Copper, lead, zinc, gold and silver are also mined. Many of Europe's mineral resources are located near industrial or population centres and are easily reached by land and water transport.

Abundant supplies of oil have been found in the North Sea around Scotland. This oil rig is at Cromarty Firth.

THE QUEST FOR ENERGY

Most of Europe's energy is supplied by power stations fuelled by coal, oil or gas. Large quantities of oil and gas are found in the North Sea, around the Caspian Sea and the northern plains of eastern Europe.

In the 1960s and 1970s many European countries developed nuclear power as an additional source of energy. But its high cost, the problem of disposal of nuclear waste and a disastrous explosion at a reactor in Chernobyl in the Ukraine in 1986, have made many nations rethink their policies towards nuclear power. In the countries of the former Soviet Union, the problems of operating and then decommissioning their ageing reactors have yet to be solved.

Natural gas is cleaner than oil and coal, but there are limits to supplies – perhaps enough to last only until the mid-2020s. The cleanest form of energy is hydroelectric power. The mountainous countries of Scandinavia, Austria and Switzerland are largely self-sufficient in energy from this source. Large dams on rivers such as the Volga, supply energy to Eastern Europe and Russia. But even hydroelectric power is not without its problems. Dams cause flooding and silting, altering the course or flow of rivers and making the installations less efficient.

■ Tin
■ Iron ore
▲ Lead
▼ Bauxite
○ Copper
● Zinc
◯ Nickel
◇ Uranium
▽ Gold
△ Silver

Above Europe's metal resources.

Below Following the nuclear reactor disaster at Chernobyl, there has been an increase in the number of people in the area suffering from cancer. This child is in the leukaemia ward of the hospital in Kiev.

PUTTING THE LID ON CHERNOBYL

A Ukrainian nuclear engineer at Chernobyl said this after the disaster: 'What could we do? We are a nation with a growing population and a poor economy. We needed more power in order to compete with the West. OK, we knew that our water-cooled reactors were not as safe as those in the West, but they refused to give us technical help when we needed it most; now they blame us for polluting their countryside! I'm the one who had to go back into that tomb of sand we built round the damaged reactor, to see what was happening. Now they give me 5 years to live.'

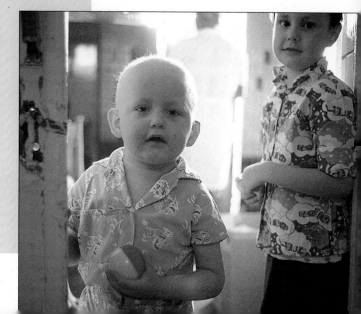

FOOD AND FARMING

Many of the world's food crops and ways of farming were first developed around the Mediterranean Sea. As urban populations grew, farming became more intensive and scientific, and productivity increased. Improved transport and better ways of preserving food meant that new markets were opened up. Now Europe is a major exporter of food as well as supplying many of its own needs.

Wheat, barley and oats are the major crops grown throughout most of Europe. The EU is one of the world's major cereal producers, accounting for 13.1 per cent of world output. Russia produces a further 14.6 per cent. Sugar beet, rye, potatoes and hay are also widespread. The growing of oilseed crops, such as sunflowers and oil-seed rape, for products like margarine, is increasing. Maize is grown in the sheltered Danube Valley and in irrigated areas of the Mediterranean. Citrus fruits, olives, grapes and soft vegetables like tomatoes are also grown there.

The grazing of livestock is common in mountainous and hilly areas as well as in the moist, low-lying pastures of Western Europe. Dairy farming is found throughout Europe, and Denmark and the Netherlands are highly specialized in pig production. Sheep are raised widely in the UK, and sheep and goats in the drier regions of the Mediterranean countries.

Eastern European countries lag behind the West in agricultural methods and machinery. These Romanian women still harvest wheat with sickles.

MOUNTAINS OF FOOD, LAKES OF WINE

Currently, Western Europe produces more food than it needs. While it is possible to give some away to countries that have insufficient food, problems of transport and storage make this difficult. A system of quotas has been introduced in the EU to limit production and to get rid of the vast 'food mountains' that have built up. Despite this, sugar surpluses rose over 25 per cent in the early 1990s. France, Italy and Spain now destroy vines which produce wine of poor quality to reduce Europe's 'wine lake'. Many people blame the EU's Common Agricultural Policy, which guarantees prices by giving subsidies. This protects farmers, especially those in poorer areas, but many think it is a wasteful system.

THROWING IT ALL AWAY

Jennifer Nicholson is a dairy farmer in Berkshire, southern England. Last year the quality of winter feed (hay and silage) was poor and Jennifer's cows actually produced less milk than her EU quota allowed. This year, with good quality feed, she has already reached her limit with 2 months to go. She is faced with the prospect of throwing away any new milk she produces or allowing her herd to 'go dry'. She says: 'It seems a crazy system when you can't even give it away.'

Items most frequently consumed by West and East Germans in 1988 (in order of volume).

WEST GERMANY	EAST GERMANY
Fishery products	Eggs
Cheese	Milk
Fresh and tropical fruits	Potatoes
Tea and coffee	Rye bread
Wine and sparkling wines	Cocoa
Non-alcoholic drinks	Sugar
Tobacco	Spirits

FOR RICHER, FOR POORER

Even if goods are produced in large quantities, high prices may prevent people from obtaining them. Look at the differences in consumption of agricultural products in East and West Germany in 1988 on the left.

In Western Europe large combine harvesters gather in the wheat crop.

Agricultural production in Europe (% of total production by value for the whole of Europe and for a number of individual countries).

TYPE OF PRODUCT	Europe	Denmark	Ireland	Italy	UK
Cereals	10.9	15.5	5.3	8.1	16.2
Root crops (potatoes, etc.)	4.6	3.4	3.0	3.2	5.9
Industrial crops (eg. oilseed)	3.6	4.8	0.2	3.9	2.8
Fresh fruit and vegetables	14.2	2.2	3.0	22.3	10.8
Wine and olive oil	7.2	0.0	0.0	9.7	0.0
Flowers/ornamental plants	3.9	5.0	0.0	4.6	2.0
Total crop production	**50.0**	**35.2**	**13.1**	**59.9**	**41.0**
Cattle	11.9	8.5	38.4	8.9	13.4
Pigs	10.4	27.4	5.6	6.4	7.7
Sheep and goats	1.9	0.1	4.4	0.7	4.6
Poultry	4.4	1.8	3.0	5.5	6.8
Milk and eggs	19.7	24.0	33.1	15.2	25.0
Total animal production	**50.0**	**64.8**	**86.9**	**39.1**	**59.0**

Source: *Europe in figures*, Eurostat 1995

LIVING FORESTS

The main commercial forest regions are the coniferous forests of Norway, Sweden, Finland and Russia. In Scandinavia, the average amount of forest per member of the population is 3 hectares, compared with 0.1 hectares in the rest of Europe. Some of the central and southern EU countries are also timber producers, particularly France, Germany and Spain.

Forests are also becoming places for leisure, recreation and education. In the UK, a number of Community Forests have been created near large urban areas to give people better access to the countryside.

Above *Logs being moved in Sweden. Most Scandinavian forestry businesses cover no more than 30-50 hectares, and are family-run.*

FOOD FROM THE SEA

Fishing is important in Europe, although only employing about 0.2 per cent of the workforce and subject to disputes among EU members and other countries. Cod and herring are the main species caught but plaice, haddock, salmon, sea trout and mackerel are also taken. Tuna and sardines are important along much of the Mediterranean coastline and off Spain and Portugal. Norway, Denmark, Spain, Iceland, Russia and the UK are the leading fishing nations – Iceland depends for 80 per cent of its exports on fishing.

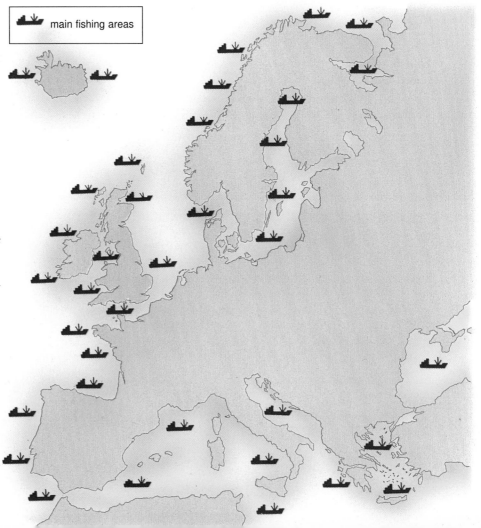

main fishing areas

Right *Fishing areas in Europe.*

Above The most productive areas for the fishing trawlers are the North Sea, the coastal waters of Norway and the areas around Iceland and Greenland.

THE LAST CATCH

Donal O'Hara was a fisherman all his life. He sailed his small fishing boat out from Galway on the west coast of Ireland every day to catch cod and whiting. Donal understood the need to limit the size of catches so that the fish would not disappear. Then the waters he felt were his by right were opened up to other European countries, with bigger, more powerful trawlers, modern detecting equipment and enormous nets. As his catches grew smaller, Donal headed further and further into the Atlantic in search of bigger shoals, but it was the beginning of the end.

Now Donal cannot make a living fishing, and he will not go to sea again. His boat, which is too small to be used for modern fishing, cannot be sold.

Europe's common fisheries policy means that all EU countries have access to waters round the continent. Because of rapidly declining fish stocks in the Atlantic and North Sea, strict quotas for size of catches are now set, but it is feared that stocks will take many years, if ever, to recover fully.

Left One possible answer to the problem of declining fish stocks is fish farming – the artificial rearing of fish or shellfish. Here, salmon are being produced on a fish farm in France. Norway alone produces 115,000 tonnes of salmon a year. The EU as a whole produces 678,000 tonnes of farmed mussels and oysters.

INDUSTRY

Until the 1980s, manufacturing employed the largest percentage of Europe's working population. Now there is a shift to the service industries, like banking, insurance and tourism. In some countries bordering the Mediterranean Sea, tourism now accounts for over half the national income. Until quite recently, the main industries were based on the processing of raw materials such as fruits, agricultural products, minerals, wood and fish. Now, they are based on the production of finished goods such as machinery, vehicles, textiles, chemicals and electrical goods, many of which are exported.

Motor manufacture is one of Germany's main industries. These cars on the BMW production line are being assembled by robots.

TRANSPORT

Transport is now a major industry in itself. It represents over 5 per cent of Europe's total economic turnover and accounts for over 5 per cent of all employment. It also represents 28 per cent of Europe's total energy consumption.

Europe has one of the densest transport networks in the world. Germany and Belgium have about 110 km of railways per 10,000 km², twice as much as Italy, France and the UK, and much higher than most of southern and Eastern Europe. Germany, the Netherlands and Belgium have the densest motorway networks (about 50 km per 1000 km²).

Main manufacturing industries in Europe, by value

- Food products 12.8%
- Electrical and electronic equipment 14.8%
- Cars, lorries, transport equipment 12.2%
- Chemicals 12%
- Machinery 10%
- Metal products 8.4%
- Textiles, clothing, leather and footwear 2.8%
- Paper, paper products, printing and publishing 7.6%
- Sand, gravel, precious stones, etc. 4.8%
- Rubber and processing of plastics 5.1%
- Metal-working industries 3.6%
- Timber and wooden furniture 3.2%
- Precision, optical and high technology instruments 1.5%
- Others 1.3%

Source: *Europe in figures*, Eurostat 1995

SUPER COMMUTER

Ulrich Christophersen is the 'new commuter'. Twice a week he flies from his office in Norway to Dortmund in Germany to conduct his international business in precision machine tools. He reckons he can achieve more in a 2 hour meeting than a week of phoning and faxes. 'Business is about people,' he says. 'I can sort out problems on the spot, make decisions and plan ahead.' By the afternoon, he is on a flight back to Oslo. 'It's just an ordinary day at the office,' he says – and he is not joking!

KEEP ON TRUCKIN'

Helene Huber is a Dutch truck driver. She drives her own Fiat articulated rig, taking 20-tonne containers from Rotterdam to other EU and Eastern European countries. Some of her journeys last up to a week and the rig is equipped like a small caravan. Border controls have now all but vanished in the EU. 'Sometimes I forget which country I'm in!' she says. The Eastern Europe borders can still be a problem though. 'They are afraid of drugs coming from the West. Last time my rig was stopped and searched in Bulgaria, I was frightened they would find something planted by dealers in Holland. It is a risk we have to take.'

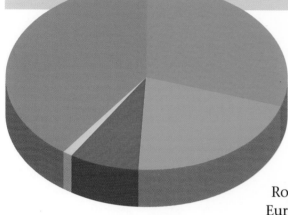

Goods transported within Europe.

- By road 38%
- By sea 26.2%
- By inland waterways (canals and rivers) 18.4%
- By rail 6.8%
- By air 0.4%

Source: *Europe in figures*, Eurostat 1995

One of the biggest changes over the past 15 years has been the transport of goods by container, which can be carried by sea and inland waterways and then unloaded onto lorries or trucks for the last part of their journey. The Rhine is navigable for 1000 km and is linked by canals to other major rivers such as the Meuse and the Elbe. Most sea transport is concentrated in about fifty ports, mainly on the North Sea and Atlantic coast. They include Rotterdam, Marseilles and Hamburg. In trade with non-European countries, 78 per cent of traffic is still carried by sea.

Air traffic is now so dense over parts of Europe that traffic control and air and noise pollution are major problems, particularly in a triangle between London, Paris and Frankfurt.

The French trains à grande vitesse (TGVs) run from Paris to other main cities at speeds of up to 300 kph. They are made up of eight or nine carriages with a locomotive at each end.

THE ENVIRONMENT

Because of the high population density and the intensity of agriculture and industry, Europe's environment is constantly under pressure. In Europe, 56 per cent of land is given over to agriculture and 30 per cent is regularly ploughed. An ever-increasing percentage of land is covered by industrial sites, recreational areas and communication networks. The need for housing continues to grow as urban areas expand.

Industrial pollution is still a major problem in many parts of Europe. In the East, where there is little money to invest in new technology, harmful emissions are particularly bad. There are also other, less obvious, effects. Increases in sewage and drainage systems mean that water is carried away directly to rivers and the sea and is no longer available to replace underground water supplies.

Left Lakes that cannot support life because of the effects of acid rain can have their acidity neutralized by the addition of lime.

RICH AND POOR

Many of these developments are designed to increase Europe's wealth and prosperity. But while many Europeans have benefited and enjoy a high standard of living, a significant minority are still poor. Some people would argue that the gap between the rich and the poor is actually increasing, even in the wealthiest countries. This applies not only to wealth itself, but to the availability of good education, adequate healthcare and proper housing. If Europe is to prosper, it has to make sure its development is sustainable; that is, that it improves the standards of living of all its people without damaging the source of its wealth – the environment.

DON'T BREATHE THE AIR

Sulphur dioxide and nitrogen dioxide from power stations and petrol vehicles are the main causes of acid rain, reacting with water high in the atmosphere and returning to earth, sometimes hundreds or even thousands of kilometres from their source. Thousands of lakes in the Scandinavian countries, receiving westerly winds from the UK and the heavily industrialized countries of Western Europe, are now devoid of all life because of their acidity. Many northern forests are now seriously damaged as a result of acid deposition (rain and snow). Carbon dioxide from the burning of fossil fuels and methane from livestock production, contribute to the greenhouse effect. Ammonia and certain complex chemicals used by industry damage the ozone layer.

Europe, particularly the EU, is acting to reduce this damage by, for example, cutting harmful emissions from power stations, making the installation of catalytic converters on new cars compulsory and encouraging the development of 'lean-burn' engines. But Europe's energy consumption and use of vehicles is itself rising, and reductions in air pollution are slow. Only by reducing the continent's energy needs and changing how Europeans live, for example by making more use of public transport and transferring more freight to the railways, can real progress be made.

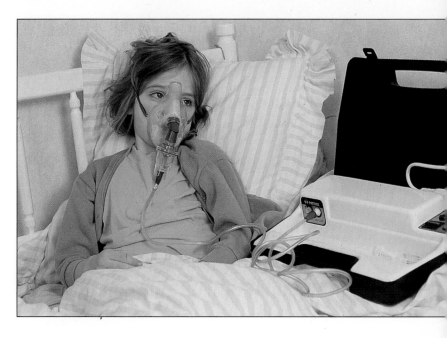

Above A 6-year-old girl lying in a hospital bed after an asthma attack. A direct effect of air pollution on human health can be seen in the increasing number of asthma attacks.

Left The generation of energy from fossil fuels, transport, agriculture and other industrial activities places a heavy burden on the atmosphere. This paper mill in Spain is producing a variety of waste products from chemical processes and the treatments involved in the manufacture of wood pulp.

WATER AND LAND

Europe's land and waterways are also affected by pollution. Water pollution comes from agriculture (eg. nitrates in fertilizers and pesticides); from domestic sources (sewage and rubbish); and from industrial processes. Often they are complex, highly toxic compounds that remain for long periods in the environment.

Above *Europe has a number of World Heritage Sites, such as the Bialoweiza National Park in Poland (shown here), the Giant's Causeway in Northern Ireland and the Danube Delta in Romania.*

Below *A discharge pipe for waste material pumps liquid on to Seaham Beach, County Durham in England.*

Main causes of extinction of different plant species in Germany (number of species affected).

Changes in land use	589
Disappearance of rare sites	255
Landfill and urbanization	247
Disappearance of wetlands	201
Enrichment of soil (fertilizers, etc.)	176
Mining and quarrying	163
Use of agricultural machinery	123
Maintenance and harnessing of rivers, etc.	68
Air and soil pollution	38
Enrichment of water (sewage, farm 'run off', etc.)	36
Use of herbicides	26

The land, too, is under pressure. There is now very little that remains of Europe's original environment. Only in the north, where there are vast areas of tundra wetland and forest, has the land remained largely untouched. Large mammals, such as wolves, bears and wild boar have disappeared from much of the continent. EU guidelines for the conservation of nature are being drawn up, but will take time to put into effect. For example, the Bird Directive now requires member states to take steps to protect over 175 species of birds and their habitats (where they live, feed or breed).

Most individual countries have their own system of nature reserves and protected areas such as National Parks or areas of particular scientific interest, but the level of protection given to these areas varies. In addition, Europe is rich in sites of international importance such as the Camargue, a vast area of wetland and marsh in southern France, and the Wash in the east of England. Both are Ramsar sites, according to the International Agreement of 1996, protected because of their importance as refuges for wildfowl (geese and ducks).

Right *Europe is rich in magnificent buildings and historic sites, but many are being rapidly eroded by air pollution. Here, laser treatment is being used to clean grime off Bordeaux Cathedral, France.*

MOVING TARGET

Peter Micallef shoots birds. He is not a cruel man by nature, but each morning in April he takes his shotgun onto the hills beyond his village in Malta and fires at thousands of songbirds migrating north. His son captures others in nets and on sticky lime twigs placed among the trees. The birds are good to eat, but are not an essential part of their diet. It is tradition, and tradition is hard to change. The Maltese government, under pressure from other parts of Europe, is pressing him to stop. But what right have they to interfere with a way of life that has gone on for generations?

EUROPE IN THE WORLD TODAY

In the past, Europe has played an important role in the world, perhaps out of all proportion to its size. Now it has a more modest role, as countries such as the USA, Japan and other rapidly developing nations of south-east Asia, become more influential.

But Europe is still important. It lies at the heart of an immense land mass that includes Africa and Asia and so continues to have an important strategic and political role in the world. The EU alone is the biggest exporter and importer of goods and services in the world; this will increase still further as some of the Eastern European countries join the Economic Union.

Europe is an important contributor of overseas aid to the so-called developing countries. The European Development Fund is designed to ensure that funding goes to useful projects and helps decrease foreign debts, while also protecting the environment. It also allows developing countries to have better access to markets within Europe. But debt repayment by these countries and interest payments on European loans, often exceed the donations given. Meanwhile, some aid organisations question whether European development funding is appropriate. Does it really help individual people and communities, or does it go into big government projects that mainly benefit European construction companies?

Above Oxfam is one of a number of European charity organisations that help developing countries. Here, clothes are being distributed to Burundian Hutu refugees.

Below A UN team installs wells and pumps in a refugee camp in Liberia.

SECURITY FOR ALL?

Europe also plays an important role in world security as part of NATO and the UN. But the end of the Cold War means that Europe is now having to review its position as a world power. One of the EU's main objectives for the coming years is to develop a foreign policy. There is already co-operation over the building of a European fighter aircraft.

The prototype European fighter aircraft, which is a joint project between several European countries.

A UNITED STATES OF EUROPE?

So what is the future for Europe? In 1986, The Single European Act created a single internal market within the EU, which removed all trade barriers so the Community became, in effect, a single trading nation. In addition, common policies over the environment and technology were agreed. In 1993, member states signed a further agreement, the Maastricht Treaty, which took European integration a step further. In 1997, a third agreement, the Treaty of Amsterdam, created new citizens' rights and targets for freedom of movement and employment. In 1999, a single European currency, called the euro, became the official currency of eleven members of the EU, including France, Germany and Italy. The currency aims to help trade both within the EU and externally.

Some people, particularly in the UK, are worried that the European Union is going too far. They are afraid that individual countries will lose their national identity and sovereignty. Perhaps the future will see a huge new superstate, made up of most of Europe, larger and more powerful than the USA.

THE NEW EUROPEANS

So is there such a person as 'a European'? The history of Europe shows how its people are the result of almost continuous movement and mixing of different populations. Yet differences and individual cultures remain. Do we want to keep these differences? Much of Europe's history has also been one of terrible wars and prolonged hardship. Can we avoid this in future by closer integration and co-operation? How do we get the balance right? These are difficult and vital questions. Your decisions, as new Europeans, will help create the answers.

TIMELINE

BC **6000** Farmers from Anatolia (now Turkey) reach Greece and Crete; farming spreads to northern and western Europe.

3000 Olives, vines and cereals cultivated in Greece; some trading abroad.

1900–1200 Civilization of Mycenae (Greece) established by Indo-Europeans migrating from the east.

753 Founding of the Roman Empire.

500 Celts from central Europe reach Spain, Britain, Ireland and the Netherlands.

336–323 Alexander the Great conquers Persia (now Iran and Iraq) and establishes the Greek Empire as far as India, but it is broken up after his death.

AD **43–117** Romans conquer Britain; Roman Empire reaches its greatest extent.

312–395 Emperor Constantine converted to Christianity; Roman Empire divided into east and west; the west declines under attack from Germanic tribes.

449–457 Angles and Saxons from central Asia invade England.

527–565 Emperor Justinian establishes Byzantine Empire around the Mediterranean, preserving Christianity through the Greek (Eastern) Orthodox Church.

700–960 Slavs (tribes of Indo-European origin) spread across eastern Europe, founding independent Slav states, including Poland, Russia, Croatia and Bulgaria.

793–800 Vikings from Scandinavia raid England; Charlemagne crowned Emperor of the Romans; his kingdom is later divided to form the basis of modern France and Germany.

871–899 Alfred the Great resists the advance of the Vikings and Danes in England; Norway established as independent country.

936–1054 Otto I of Germany conquers Italy and founds the Holy Roman Empire (Roman Catholic Church). Split (schism) between the Eastern Orthodox Church and the Western (Catholic) Church.

1096–1204 Byzantine Empire defeated by Turkish Muslims; Christians embark on Crusades. Despite the wars, trade links between east and west established.

1237–1241 Mongols from Northern Russia under Genghis Khan establish large empire, threatening Europe and Asia.

1337–1453 Hundred Years War between England and France, ending in English defeat. Black Death (bubonic plague) kills one third of Europe (1347–1351).

1389–1453 Ottomans overthrow the Byzantine Empire.

1400–1500 The Renaissance, a period rich in literature and art, blooms in Europe.

1515–1534 Spanish conquistadors attack Mexico and Peru, destroying the Aztec and Inca civilizations

1517–1603 Reforms to the Roman Catholic Church, led by Martin Luther, lead to the Reformation and the creation of the Protestant Church in western Europe.

1600–1700 Europeans establish colonies in other continents. The decline of the Ottoman Empire and Spain.

1618–1648 Thirty Years War involves most western European powers. Sweden, France and Brandenburg-Prussia (later Germany) emerge strengthened.

1650–1750 The Age of Reason or Enlightenment – a new respect for science and learning sweeps Europe.

1762–1796 Russia exerts increasing influence over eastern Europe. Advances in science and technology mark the beginning of the Industrial Revolution. The French

Revolution (1789) begins; France becomes a republic and declares war on Austria and Prussia. Abolition of slavery. French troops, led by Napoleon Bonaparte, conquer much of Italy and Switzerland.

1813–1815 Napoleon defeated at the Battle of Waterloo by Britain and Prussia.

1850–1871 Prussia expands its territories to form a large united Germany under Kaiser Wilhelm I. Russia goes to war with Britain, France and Turkey over its claims over Turkey (Crimean War). Karl Marx publishes *Das Kapital* (1867) and establishes the ideas of communism.

1877–1914 Most of Africa colonized by European powers. Germany forms an alliance with Austria-Hungary and Italy. Kaiser Wilhelm II encourages further expansion of Germany.

1908–1914 Unrest between Balkan countries and Austria-Hungary; the assassination of the crown prince of Austria by a Serbian triggers the First World War.

1917 Russian revolt against the ruling Tsar (Russian Revolution); Bolshevik party set up a communist regime.

1918 Germany surrenders to the allies; new nations become independent – the Baltic republics (Latvia, Estonia and Lithuania), Czechoslovakia and Yugoslavia.

1919 League of Nations set up to help preserve world peace.

1923–1925 USSR formed. National Socialism (Fascism) emerges in Germany under Adolf Hitler and in Italy under Benito Mussolini.

1930–1935 In Russia, Stalin forces state ownership. Capitalist Europe enters the Great Depression. Fascist parties come to power in Italy, Germany and Spain. Germany begins the forced repatriation, and then murder of 'foreign nationals' and others, particularly communists and Jews.

1939–1945 Hitler invades Czechoslovakia and Poland; Mussolini seizes Albania. Britain and France declare war on Germany and the Second World War begins. Germany finally defeated on 8 May 1945 and split into occupation zones.

1945–9 Europe divided into Eastern (Communist) and Western Blocs. Formation of NATO. European countries lose most of their overseas colonial powers

1955–1956 Soviet Union signs the Warsaw Pact. Unrest in Hungary crushed by USSR.

1957–1960 Treaty of Rome establishes the Common Market (EEC). Cyprus gains independence, but remains divided on Greek/Turkish lines.

1961 East Germany builds the Berlin Wall.

1968 Revival of unrest in Northern Ireland between Protestants and Catholics.

1980–85 Unrest in Poland led by Lech Walesa. Popular protests against nuclear weapons. USSR President Gorbachev introduces *perestroyka* (restructuring) and *glasnost* (openness).

1989–1990 Poland and Hungary elect democratic governments. Popular uprisings in Czechoslovakia, East Germany and Bulgaria restore democracy, but in Romania there is a bloody revolt. Berlin Wall demolished and East and West Germany united.

1991–1995 Czechoslovakia divides into Slovakia and the Czech Republic. Yugoslavia torn by ethnic conflict.

1992 Maastricht Treaty signed by twelve European Community members and the European Union (EU) is formed.

1995 Sweden, Austria and Finland join the EU. War ends in Croatia. New Yugoslavia formed from Serbia and Montenegro.

1998 Conflict and violence in Kosovo.

1999 Launch of the euro (European single currency).

GLOSSARY

Administration How a country or organization is run or managed.

Alliance Grouping of countries or regions co-operating for mutual benefit, eg. protection, economic advantage.

Balkans Region of Europe making up most of former Yugoslavia, Albania, Bulgaria, Greece, Romania and part of Turkey; often known for unrest between its nations.

Capitalism Form of economy depending heavily on competition and private ownership of industry, with little interference by the state or government.

Commodity Any article or product that can be traded.

Coniferous Trees, such as pine and spruce, that keep their leaves in winter; also known as softwoods.

Consumer goods Products that people buy in shops, eg. electrical goods and ceramics.

Culture Aspects of a country or society that make it distinctive – its way of life, art, music and religion.

Decommission To take out of use; often refers to nuclear plants where the safe dismantling and storage of nuclear reactors and waste is very costly and difficult.

Discrimination To treat different groups (eg. ethnic or religious groups) differently, usually to their disadvantage.

Deciduous Trees that shed their leaves in winter; also known as hardwoods.

Democratic System of government or decision-making through a voting system open to all.

Domestic needs What a country needs in terms of goods and materials to satisfy the requirements of its own people.

Economy System of production of goods and services; distribution of income, exchange with other countries and consumption.

Emissions Discharges of waste (often pollutant) materials from industrial or other processes.

Fascism Form of government promoting extreme nationalism and oppression of other groups or beliefs.

Federation Close association of states or regions, eg. the States of America; some people fear that European countries will become federation of member states belonging to the 'super state' of Europe.

Free market Economic system in which trade and commerce are not restricted or controlled by government.

Greenhouse effect Warming of the earth's atmosphere caused by the build up of certain gases, particularly carbon dioxide.

Holocaust Mass extermination of Jews by the Nazis before and during the Second World War.

Ideological Beliefs based on political convictions, eg. communism or capitalism.

Integration Merging of peoples, cultures or economies.

Intensive farming Farming involving high concentrations of animals or wide-spread use of agricultural chemicals.

Investment Money spent by governments, industry or individuals to support development of a product or service; a 'return' on the investment is usually expected.

Legislation National or international laws.

Over-regulation Where there is too much control over ways in which things are done.

Peat Vegetable matter that does not decompose but remains as a fibrous material in marshy or boggy areas; it is often extracted for fuel or as a soil improver.

Peninsula Area of land, largely surrounded by water.

Persecution Unjust or brutal treatment of a person or group because of their race, beliefs, religion or colour.

Plateau Large, flat area of land, usually at altitude.

Political union System of government in which a number of countries share common policies and a degree of central control.

Privatization Selling off of state-owned industry to private investment (private ownership).

Resources Usually naturally occurring materials available to a country, eg. coal, iron ore, forests or fish.

Republic A country that has no monarchy and therefore often has a president and a prime minister.

Sanctions Penalties, eg. trade restrictions, placed on one country by others to force it to co-operate in a particular way, eg. over the treatment of minority groups.

Single currency Proposed system, whereby all countries in the EU have the same currency and monetary system.

Sovereignty A country's right to determine its own affairs.

Standard of living Level of wealth and services available to citizens, in terms of education, healthcare, goods, etc.

Stockpile Usually refers to the build up of large quantities of weapons, particularly nuclear weapons.

Subsidy Payment, usually by government, to support a particular activity, eg. farming.

Urbanized Where a large proportion of the population is concentrated in towns and cities.

Weathering Processes by which rocks and landscape are changed by wind, rain, etc.

FURTHER INFORMATION

NON-FICTION FOR CHILDREN

Armistice, 1918 (The World Wars series) (Hodder Wayland, 2000)

The Berlin Wall (New Perspectives series)(Hodder Wayland, 1999)

Chernobyl and other Nuclear Accidents East Africa (New Perspectives series) (Hodder Wayland, 1999)

Eastern Europe (World Fact Files series)(Hodder Wayland, 1998)

France (Country Fact Files series)(Hodder Wayland, 1997)

Germany (Country Fact Files series)(Hodder Wayland, 1997)

Germany and Japan Attack (The World Wars series) (Hodder Wayland, 2000)

Great Battles of World War II (The World Wars series) (Hodder Wayland, 2000)

Leaders of World War II (The World Wars series) (Hodder Wayland, 2000)

My Childhood in Nazi Germany (Hodder Wayland, 1994)

The Rise of the Nazis (New Perspectives series)(Hodder Wayland, 1999)

Russia (Country Fact Files series)(Hodder Wayland, 1997)

Spain (Country Fact Files series)(Hodder Wayland, 1997)

Sweden (Country Fact Files series)(Hodder Wayland, 1997)

United Kingdom (Country Fact Files series)(Hodder Wayland, 1997)

The War in Former Yugoslavia (New Perspectives series)(Hodder Wayland, 1999)

The War in Kosovo (New Perspectives series)(Hodder Wayland, 1999)

The War in the Trenches (The World Wars series) (Hodder Wayland, 2000)

World War II: The Allied Victory (The World Wars series) (Hodder Wayland, 2000)

WEBSITES

The European Union: http://europa.eu.int

United Nations: http://www.undp.org

NON FICTION REFERENCE MATERIAL

Philips Geographical Digest 2000 (Heinemann Educational, 2000)

FILMS

The European film industry produces a huge number of feature films each year, many of which are available on video.

Among the most popular films concerned with Britain's colonial history and the Victorian age are those produced by Merchant-Ivory. *Howard's End* is the story of the relationship between two families, which centres around a house in the countryside. *A Passage to India* is about the relationship between the British and Indians in India during the late nineteenth century, and what happens to a young Indian doctor when he falls foul of Imperial India. Both films are based on novels by EM Forster.

INDEX

The figures in **bold** refer to photographs